MW01601339

THE
OVERLOOKED
BUILT FROM THE
CONCRETE
DIANE WHITE

THE OVERLOOKED

Built From the Concrete

By: Diane White

First Edition 2025

Copyright © 2025 by Diane White

All rights reserved.
ISBN: 979-8-218-90435-7
First Edition: 2025
Printed in the United States of America
No part of this book may be reproduced, distributed, or transmitted in any form or by any means electronic, mechanical, photocopying, recording, or otherwise—without the prior written permission of the author, except for brief quotations used in reviews or as permitted under applicable copyright law.

This book is a work of nonfiction based on the author's personal experiences, memories, and reflections. Certain names, identifying details, locations, and events have been changed or omitted to protect the privacy of individuals. Some scenes, dialogue, and timelines have been reconstructed from memory for narrative clarity. While every effort has been made to portray events truthfully, memory is subjective and others may recall events differently.

Brief references to song lyrics, music, scripture, and other cultural works are used for purposes of commentary, reflection, and personal storytelling. Such references are not intended to reproduce or substitute the original works and are believed to fall under fair use. All referenced works remain the property of their respective copyright holders. Scripture quotations are used for inspirational and reflective purposes. Biblical references may be paraphrased or quoted from public-domain translations or credited modern translations where applicable.

This book is an original work authored by Diane White and is based primarily on the author's lived experiences, personal memories, and original written material.

Any references to public events, cultural moments, music, scripture, or widely known phrases are included solely for purposes of commentary, reflection, and narrative context. Such references are brief, transformative, and non-substitutive, and are believed to fall within the scope of fair use under U.S. copyright law.

No copyrighted works including song lyrics, poems, or written texts are reproduced in full. Where lyrics, scripture, or quotations are referenced, they are either paraphrased, limited to short excerpts, or drawn from public-domain sources.

All trademarks, service marks, song titles, artist names, and referenced works remain the property of their respective owners. Their inclusion does not imply endorsement, sponsorship, or affiliation. The author asserts full authorship and ownership of the original content contained in this book. This book is an original work authored by Diane White and is based primarily on the author's lived experiences, personal memories, and original written material.

Sources & Legal Notice

This book is an original work authored by Diane White and is based primarily on the author's lived experiences, personal memories, and original written material.

Any references to public events, cultural moments, music, scripture, or widely known phrases are included solely for purposes of commentary, reflection, and narrative context. Such references are brief, transformative, and non-substitutive, and are believed to fall within the scope of fair use under U.S. copyright law.

No copyrighted works including song lyrics, poems, or written texts are reproduced in full. Where lyrics, scripture, or quotations are referenced, they are either paraphrased, limited to short excerpts, or drawn from public-domain sources.

All trademarks, service marks, song titles, artist names, and referenced works remain the property of their respective owners. Their inclusion does not imply endorsement, sponsorship, or affiliation. The author asserts full authorship and ownership of the original content contained in this book.

Dedication

*For the ones they didn't see coming.
For my daughters' proof that strength has a
heartbeat. This book is dedicated to the women
who stood beside me, the children who gave me
purpose, and the God who never let go, even when
I didn't know how to hold on.*

Author's Note

This isn't fiction.
This isn't polished for comfort.
Every word you're about to read was lived.
The names may change, but the truth remains
untouched. These stories come from the same girl
who had to grow up too fast, the same woman who
kept showing up even when her soul was tired.
I wrote this for the ones who've been through too
much to ever tell it all, the ones who've cried in
silence, laughed in pain, and loved through loss. I
wrote it for the women who are still trying to find
themselves after life took something they can
never get back.
This book is proof that broken crayons still color,
that God really does use the overlooked, and that
strength doesn't always show up loud. Sometimes
it whispers, "I'm still here."
So, before you turn the page, let me say this plain:
I didn't write this to impress you. I wrote this to
free me.
And maybe, just maybe, to free someone else too.
— Diane White

Table of Contents

Preface: "Rose in Harlem" Moment

October 25, 2025. "Rose in Harlem" by Teyana Taylor blasting through my 2016 Nissan Altima. Windows cracked, wind kissing my cheeks, mind somewhere in the clouds just enjoying the fruits of my labor.

The beat dropped, and that line hit me deep: "Been through more than a lil' bit… had to get it out the soil." Whew. I felt that.

Then she said: "It be the ones, the ones you closest to. It be the ones, the ones you trust, them too.

It be the ones, the ones you look up to. It be the ones… Don't get caught up, young girl."And right there, I knew this one's for you.

To my African American women. To my Black women. To my HBCU-made women. And I can't forget my moms, the teen moms, the single moms, and even the "ain't-shhh" moms (you know who you are).

This is for my overlooked women, my distant aunties, the babies of the bunch, and the most loyal souls in the room. Stay a while, because I

promise you everything I'm about to say happened. And I mattered.
If you've never heard it before, hear it now: YOU MATTER.
When you're chosen, your trials and tribulations start looking like scripture, except you're walking it out in real time. It's not until you finally let God use you that you see... it was truly all in His plan.

Bridge I
The Concrete and the Calling

There were moments I cried out, "Lord, I don't understand why You're letting me fall when the world is in Your hands."

But I learned that sometimes God lets you walk through the valley because there's something you need to gain on the journey. The concrete that tried to break me was the very thing God used to build me. This book is for every woman who has been counted out or cast aside. For the ones who are both soft and strong. For the mothers moving mountains for their babies. For the educators pouring into other people's children. For the loyal women whose hearts have been broken but still beat with hope.

If you see yourself in these pages, know that I see you too. I'm going to tell my truth the raw, unpolished, sometimes painful truth because there's purpose in it. Maybe it will speak to the purpose in you.

Imagine me sitting with you, holding your hand as we take this journey together. In these pages you'll find my heart, my faith, my laughter, and the strategies that helped me fight for my soul. So, thank you, truly, for giving me a chance and listening. We're just two friends sitting on a front porch with some sweet tea or maybe a glass of wine, talking about life. You'll probably gasp, laugh, and say "same, girl" more than once.

Chapter 1
From Dirt to Concrete

The dirt can be manipulated as many times as you need. You can scoop it, pack it, water it, turn it over, reshape it repeatedly. Dirt does not fight back. It was made to be moved. But concrete... Once that foundation is poured and it dries, it is set. It is sure. It is unbothered by hands that once shaped it. Any attempt to alter it requires breaking something and that something will not be me. For a long time, I was the dirt. I was the foundation others stood on, leaned on, cried on. I was the voice of reason, the steady one, the one with answers, the woman who kept showing up even when her soul was tired. People planted themselves in my life and used my heart like soil (molding, digging, reshaping) and I let them. Not because I was weak. But because God gave me a heart that loves hard, forgives fast, and sees people where they could be, not just where they are.

So, I stayed in rooms God told me to leave. I tried to hold friendships that expired long before I let them go. I tried to be everything to everyone while quietly becoming nothing to myself. It was not until I sat with myself no noise, no audience, no title, no armor and said,

"I will not be moved by emotion anymore."

"I am done shrinking to fit into places that cannot contain me."

"I am done pretending I am still dirt when God already poured concrete over my life."

That moment in the car… that breath shaking, heart cracking, soul quiet moment… was not the first time I felt God tugging me to tell my story. But it was the moment I realized I had to. I was sitting there with my hands on the wheel, tears forming but tired of falling. And all I could whisper was, "God… I am tired. I have tried my way. Here I am." And just like that, heaven leaned in. Because sometimes God waits until you have no strength left to pretend. Sometimes your surrender is the deliverance.

*Sometimes your **"Yes"** is the key that unlocks the life you were meant to live. That **Yes** changed everything. I did not start writing as a writer. I started writing as a woman trying to breathe. Just me, my thoughts, and my open late at night after my kids finally fell asleep. Scared. Unpolished. Unsure. But writing anyway because something in my spirit refused to stay silent. Every paragraph*

*was a prayer. Every sentence was pain speaking
truth. Every line was survival with a little bit of
hope sprinkled on top. I wrote for the women who
hold the world together but fall apart in the
shower.*

*The women who smile in public and crumble in
private. The women whose strength is loud but
whose suffering is quiet. Before the bloom there
was dirt. But even dirt is home for seeds. My
beginning did not look like a beginning. It looked
like bills piling up, heartbreak sitting heavy, grief
that did not ask for permission, exhaustion in my
bones. It looked like teaching through tears,
grading papers through headaches, and still
cooking dinner when disappearing felt easier.
I learned to forgive people who should have loved
me better. And to forgive myself for loving them
longer than I should have. I learned that my peace
is not a group project. That my boundaries are not
up for discussion. That I do not have to beg for a
seat at a table God never meant for me to fit at.
So, I built my own table and invited women who
talk with their hands, pray from their belly, love
with intention, and show up with grace. Yes, they
are watching. Every step. Every blessing. Every
elevation. But intimidation always shows up when*

God starts lifting you. Keep being you just not to your abusers. The tests are part of your testimony. And I stand as living proof that God will never leave nor forsake you because His Word says, "When you pass through the waters I will be with you and through the rivers they shall not overflow you."

Not if. When. He knew the flood was coming. He also knew I would survive it. Baby the branches may break... but the roots the God planted God watered God protected roots they will hold. And this right surrender this soil this shifting this breaking this rising was the beginning of my bloom.

Chapter 2
My White is Really Black the Child They Did Not Choose

People hear "White" and swear they already know my story. Cute. I am Diane Francis White, born in Washington, D.C., raised in Prince George's County Maryland, with a name that made teachers pause like they expected a ponytail, pearls, and a mother who packed cucumber sandwiches on wheat bread. Then I would raise my brown hand and say "Present." My white is really Black.

As in clap back with scripture and a side eye Black.

As in thick and fine and quick with my mouth, not to be smart but to be truthful. Right is right. Wrong is wrong and I have never been afraid to say it. Identity, please. I learned code switching before I learned long division. I could roll my R's when Auntie called, then straighten my back when the principal walked by. Both were me. Both were true. Both were survival.

My home had gospel on Sundays, R&B on Saturdays, and carryout on Fridays. White on my mail. Black in my bones.

I was overlooked early, the youngest, the one folks forgot to call, the kid who walked into rooms already taken up by conversations I was never included in. But being overlooked taught me peace.

Nobody sees you building by the time they notice, the house already has windows.

I wrote in marble notebooks about grief, my father's addiction, laughter and loss. I wrote prayers that sounded like breath. "My white is really Black" became my way of saying: I am not what you think. I am not what tried to break me. I am what God said. Period. Let me take you back. I am the youngest of four and I will give you a glimpse of the truth I was living. My mother had me at thirty-seven. My siblings were twenty, seventeen, and ten. Two older sisters. One older brother. And then me, the bonus baby nobody planned for, and everybody had an opinion about it.

I was a bastard child point blank. My daddy was married to my sister's mother, and he had a drug addiction. Before I even awakened on earth God used chaos to birth something great.

I will be honest when it comes to anything about my dad. I know he loved me from the stories I have heard. But I also know he was selfish. Most drug addicts are. That is not shade. That is truth!
I grew up with just my mama's side because my mother never disclosed much about my father's family except that they did not like her and that her mere voice on a voicemail made one of them claim she caused a panic attack. Baby be serious. My father's mother's husband accused my mother of disturbing the peace because my daddy's voice was on our machine. Child the drama.
Honestly it was all petty B.S. if you ask me. His family favored my sister and her mother and in fairness they should have, they were married. But I was the innocent child who had to be punished for the decisions of two adults. How messed up is that? This was my life. I grew up in the shadows. This is where overlooked began. Not because I was not worthy but because sometimes people are too broken to see the blessing God placed in front of them.
My nickname was Mooda and let my family tell me that it was the only name they knew. And that is the thing about names, sometimes the one you are given hurts but the one you grow into heals. I did not know it then, but God was shaping identity out

of the pieces of a story I did not choose. I always wanted my mother to change my name. I was about five when I vividly remember her saying, "Your daddy picked your name." And me being who I am I said, "The man dead and the family don't fool with me anyway." Just like that. Imagine being overlooked by the people who were supposed to love you. Do you think a 5-year-old understands infidelity? No, all they understand is you're not wanted. Honestly, I'm glad I never got to meet, or get attached to any of my father's family.

*Yes, I know some of them well but honestly God was protecting me from more hurt, drama, and chaos. I'm grateful because any **FAMILY** that will cause a child to suffer ain't nothing I want to be a part of! It's sad because I carry a last name, I don't know any real history about, but the blessing is the name helped me identify my story. I get to tell it unapologetically and I don't owe anyone anything! I get to say exactly what I feel, and can't nobody do anything about it because it's **MY TRUTH** !*

My white was really Black. My childhood was pain wrapped in humor. My family was a lesson before it was a blessing.

Literally I've served my whole life trying to help others have a great day because I know the life I've been living, I see how the world isn't kind, they overlook the great people every day. I choose to make others smile because I've resided in darkness. I choose to joke, play, and laugh because let's be for real **LIFE** *serious enough. My purpose is to lead with love to show you all genuine true love, no strings attached, no gimmicks, no scams and see before I've ever discovered this, the enemy tried to abort it before it ever formed, but* **GOD** *said "no weaponed formed against me* **SHALL** *Prosper" and that very thing has been born. I said all of that to say To the* **OVERLOOKED** *be glad they did! You have had time to mature, develop, perfect, enhance, build, and structure.*

Who you already are Divine and wonderfully made, they saw you even before they knew you, because the light you carry can't be copied. They mock it, they try to bring others down, they truly admire you, they want to be you, but they can't because they don't know how to be themselves.
I don't hold any animosity, I hold accountability.

CHAPTER 3
BEFORE THE BLOOM

I did not just come from struggle. But struggle sat at our table more nights than comfort did. I came from laughter, from fried chicken and incense, from corner-store jokes and cracked-window gospel. We laughed loud; belly laughs that made you slap the couch. We did not have much, but joy did not cost a thing.

*We did not go to Disney. We made a theme park out of the corner store, my niece and I walking in like **CEOs**, pushing the door open where the bell chimed like applause. Plexiglass window with faded pictures of wings and happy hour combos taped to the glass, menu letters missing like teeth, but we knew our order by heart. Three-piece fried hard, extra crispy, mambo sauce, salt, pepper, ketchup; the kind of meal that made a kid feel rich. I was that kid who always spoke up not to be slick, just to be fair. If you skipped me, I said it. If you lied on my cousin, I said it. If the numbers did not add up, I said it with my chest and my pencil. I was not trying to be grown I was trying to be* *honest. I didn't know the word boundaries, but I had practice. Truth lived in my mouth early. People thought I was loud because my spirit was big, but what they missed was that I was a listener first. I studied rooms like a map. I read the temperature before I read the text. That is why people came to me for advice even when I was a kid. They knew I would tell the truth, but I knew how to put a blanket on it so it wouldn't feel cold. As a little girl my mama would say, "Be seen, not heard," and I never knew how God would use me, but I always knew He was with me. I restarted my life so many times I should've earned airline miles. But God kept catching me mid-fall, setting me down like, "Get back up, I'm not done." And still, I can't pretend the struggle wasn't real. Some days surviving felt heavier than living. I grew up with my oldest sister's kids, a niece four years older, a nephew two years older, and another niece two years under me. If I'm being honest, they were my true siblings. My sisters and I lived similar lives, just at different angles. They had my mother when she was young, I had her when she was tired. Both versions held trauma, just different colors of it. When you're the curse breaker, life doesn't hand you softness.*

My childhood felt normal until I grew old enough to realize it wasn't. My mother did the best she knew how. I was the one who held her accountable. From being a baby to six years old I was spoiled, a mama's baby her shadow.

Then life showed itself. My mama worked nights at the post office, eleven to seven, steady, consistent, always moving. I stayed home with my brother or at my oldest sister's house. Through exhaustion and bills and grief my mama still got up and worked. My sisters did too. If she didn't teach us anything else, she taught us work ethics.

After my father died, my mama got us a house, a split-level single-family home, four bedrooms, two baths, garage, yard, a cul-de-sac from section eight to keys in her hand at thirty-eight. Four kids by four fathers. Only my oldest sister's father stayed present. For the rest of us, all we knew was her.

My mother was creative, talented, hands-on. She didn't play about school. She didn't tolerate disrespect. And me? I was quick with my mouth, so she got creative: pinched the back of my arm, held my nose, washed my mouth with soap. Lessons you don't forget. She gave people places to stay. She fed people with no food. She showed up. She was a giver even when she needed giving.

I played sports, rode bikes normal things. But I also saw things kids shouldn't see people shoot up, smoke weed, drown in liquor, women abused, men abusing. By seven, I knew right from wrong. I was an auntie before I was born, so, it was strange taking orders from kids older than me, but I respected elders even if they were only elders by age.

And through it all there was my brother. My "father figure" without the title. Active. Present. Protective. My biggest headache and my shield. He annoyed me and saved me. He stood in a gap he never asked for but filled anyway. Before I tell you how he died, you must know how he lived. You must know him to understand the hole he left.

Bridge II
Rearranged the House

Grief rearranged my house without asking. Grief is hands on the knees. Grief is "what do you need?" When there is nothing. Grief turned me into an archivist overnight hoarding voice notes and blinking at pictures like they could blink back. If you know, you know, you don't get over it; you grow around it!
Now when I laugh, he's in it. When I tell the truth, he's in it. When I refuse to fold, he's in it. Love doesn't stop; it shifts from body to memory, from presence to pulse. But somewhere between holding on and healing, I lost myself. I was alive, but I wasn't me. Grief didn't just break me; it blurred me. Before healing had a name, before faith had roots, there was a night that split everything I knew clean in half. The light in me dimmed that night. The girl who laughed loud started whispering her prayers. I didn't know what trauma was yet, but I knew pain when it moved in and refused to leave.

That night is where my silence started. Where my trust cracked. Where the dirt turned heavy and my bloom almost didn't make it.

Chapter 4
The Night Everything Split

"Some nights don't just hurt you; they rearrange your whole bloodline." I was in fifth grade glowing in my little universe. Honor roll. Finally got the phone I begged for. Not prepaid. Not borrowed. Mine. I earned it with that four point zero and I took pictures with that tiny camera like the world was already watching me.

Me. My brother Joseph. Wendy, his forever girl. We didn't know those would be our last photos together. We didn't know we were capturing the end of something holy. That night started like nothing. Mama was at work on the night shift steady and exhausted but clocking in like she always did.

Joseph was supposed to come home and watch us, but he never made it. So, we slept over Shirley's apartment.

Kids scattered on couches and floors, cartoons humming low, leftover noodles still on the stove. A safe night. A regular night.

The last night before everything broke. Then the phone rang. Not a normal ring. The wrong one.

*Loud and sharp like it already knew it was
carrying death in its throat.*

*Wendy was screaming that Joseph got shot. We
jumped awake, heart racing before our eyes even
opened. Shirley grabbed her purse, grabbed her
keys, grabbed the edges of her sanity.*

*She and my sisters drove to Mama's job in the
middle of her shift because news like that cannot
be told over the phone. It must be looked at in the
face. By the time Mama walked through the door
she already knew. A mother feels death before it is
spoken. They said Joseph had been shot on Ritchie
Road in District Heights. Twenty years old. One
month and one day before his twenty first
birthday. They rushed him to the Air Force base
hospital. That's where the world started splitting.
Tammy lived in Forest Creek then, barely ten
minutes from the base. Close enough to know the
roads by heart. Close enough to feel like she
should have been able to reach him. And she was
military.*

*Her status got her through the gate, onto the base,
but access isn't the same as entry into the room.
They didn't know she was his sister, so they told
her nothing. No name. No status. No updates. She
was not allowed to see him.*

*Meanwhile back at the house in the phone
patiently waiting. Silence is too heavy to mistake.
Shirley shaking her head "no" then vocalizing it
with pain, the ending without being allowed to
witness the fight.*

*And at that moment the family split. Not just from
grief but from the way grief arrived.*

*Fast. Violent. Unfair. Random. Cruel. Joseph
wasn't just my brother. He was my almost father.
My protector. If Mama put him out, I slid the key
under the mat. He was a giant, protective teddy
bear, flawed, gifted, and a real Forrest Creek
hood legend.*

A true thug with a soft spot.

*Everybody respected him, and by default they
respected me, his fat little sister tagging behind
like his shadow.*

*My brother was smart, too smart. He didn't get in
trouble because he was bad; he got in trouble
because he was bored.*

*Regular schools couldn't hold him. Mama and he
used to argue like they were in a rap battle. He
swore he was the next 2Pac and blasted *Dear
Mama* every time he got caught doing something
dumb.*

*That boy would do the most ridiculous things and
still make them funny. He'd steal our mom's car,*

swear he was just going around the block, and
bring me with him so I couldn't snitch.
I'd be in the passenger seat, seat belt crooked, of
course being honest awww mommy going beat
your a**, and he telling me shut up as he turned
three six mafia's chicken head up through her
Lincoln town car.
But that was us chaos, love, and laughter. Those
were the days. And that's the thing about grief; it
doesn't care how real somebody was. It just takes.
One minute he's there, cracking jokes and eating
cereal out of the box. The next, he's a headline.
Twenty years old.
One month and one day before his twenty-first
birthday. Wrong place. Wrong time. An argument
that wasn't even his. And when he died that
tension snapped. The foundation cracked. People
who supported each other became secretive.
Holding anger. Holding distance. Some broke
outward, loud and reckless. Some broke inward,
quiet and unreachable.
Some drifted. Some hardened. Some shattered.
And me, I folded into myself. A little Black girl
watching her whole world fall like dominoes
starting at the head of the table. We survived
technically. But we were never the same. Joseph's
death didn't just hurt us. It unmade us. That night

didn't just split our family. It split our story.
Before Joseph. After Joseph. Two different worlds.
Two different versions of all of us.

Chapter Five
Things I Never Wanted to Say Out Loud

After Joseph died, life didn't pause for us to catch our breath. Mama fell into depression so deep the house felt darker even when the lights were on. A year went by then gradually she began to move, work, start to exist again. but it was like she was underwater and the world was muffled around her.

When she finally started trying to be present again, she went around family more, cards, gambling nights, laughter too loud for the pain we were all holding.

Adults drinking. Kids running around. A house full of people who loved to talk, but not about the things that mattered.

That's where it happened. Where I should've been protected. Where innocence should've been safe. Someone I trusted, someone I looked up to became creepy. Little touches, too close, eyes that felt wrong. A shift you feel in your spirit before you understand in your mind. And when it happened, he told me: "No one will believe you."

And for a while, I believed that lie more than I believed in myself. I was a child. But shame doesn't care about age. I felt dirty for something I didn't ask for. I replayed it repeatedly like my body didn't know how to forget.

Weekends at my uncle's house, which should've been fun, turned into panic hidden behind a straight face.

And then one day God stepped in the room. My boyfriend at the time walked in and up the stairs. Saw it with his own eyes. No explaining. No misunderstanding. Just truth exposed in real time. He looked at me and asked what had been going on. Not angry at me, concerned. Soft. Like he could see the part of me I thought I hid well. I told him enough for him to understand. He didn't ask why I didn't scream. He didn't judge me. He just believed me. His mother believed me too. She spoke up. She advocated. She didn't whisper, she said something. She made sure eyes opened even if mouths didn't want to speak. And no, it didn't end the way I imagined. No big scene, no justice served, no perfect ending.

But it didn't stay hidden. A conversation happened. The truth came out of the dark. Even though it still hurt, I know God was protecting me.

Watching me. Guiding me when I felt unprotected.
Covering me even when I didn't have words.
What changed in me after that, something inside
me went quiet. Not gone, just quieter, like my
spirit started whispering instead of laughing. I
realized my protector was gone. Joseph wasn't
there to fight for me. To step in. To say, "not my
sister." Losing him meant losing that shield, and
life wasted no time proving it. I felt alone. In a
room full of family, alone. Surrounded by noise,
alone. I blamed myself in the way only a child
knows how.
If I didn't fight, was it my fault?
If I didn't tell you, did I let it happen? Shame
taught me things God never intended. I stopped
trusting men. I flinched at touches. I avoided
hugging. I read intentions like warnings. Except
my boyfriend. He was gentle where the world was
rough. Safe where others felt dangerous. He saw
me, not just the smile, but the wound behind it.
That moment didn't just hurt me, it changed me. It
made me grow up fast.
Not years emotionally.
Spiritually.
Survival mode young.
I didn't heal at that age, I adapted.
I learned silence as protection.

I learned strength through numbness.
I learned to carry pain like it was part of growing up.
On paper I was still doing good, honor roll, phone in hand, pictures in my little camera like life was normal.
But inside I was different.
A little girl with an adult-sized scar.
Learning to smile with a story she couldn't speak yet.
Because in my family...we didn't talk about pain. We survived it.

Bridge III
Growing Up Didn't Wait for Me

Growing up didn't wait for me to be ready; it just showed up. Responsibility became my normal before childhood had even finished introducing itself.

By 13, I was babysitting Tammy's four kids: my nieces and nephews. Not occasionally, not when I felt like it, but often.

My mom was in the house, but not always present. She was battling her own storms, working, grieving, surviving. So, stepping in became second nature for me.

And don't get it twisted. I loved those kids. We laughed, played, watched TV, ate snacks, yelled at video games, all the chaotic kid stuff. They clung to me, followed me, trusted me. I was the fun aunt, the responsible one, the go-to kid raising kids right next to me, even though I was still one myself.

Every two weeks I got $100, and instead of blowing it like most 13-year-olds would, I paid my own phone bill. Thirteen with a bill. Thirteen with *responsibilities bigger than my age. Thirteen holding a piece of adulthood without knowing what to call it.*

Family wasn't a word. It was work. *You help because that's what we do. No schedule. No "let me think about it." Just show up. Always. And I did because love lived in service in my family. But even in all that responsibility, God gave me one soft place to land: Kevin.*

Kevin was my break from growing up too fast. With him, I got to be 13 again. No babysitting. No duties. Just butterflies and giggles. Matching outfits like we were famous. Amusement park dates. Staying on the phone until we fell asleep with the line still open. Inside jokes no one else understood. He made me feel seen, not for what I did, but for who I was.

There were days I'd be watching the kids, making them plates, keeping order in a house full of little voices and he'd text something goofy that had me smiling like nothing else mattered. He was laughter in the middle of responsibility. A pause button when life was pressing play too fast. God knew what He was doing giving me responsibility to mature me but love to remind me I was still a child. Growing up early built my strength. I didn't even believe I was pregnant at first.

Sex was like a family secret, whispered about, joked around, but never explained. I was a kid doing grown things without grown understanding. And then reality hit me in the face. I was fifteen… and pregnant. But even in the confusion, something in my spirit wasn't scared of the baby just the situation.

If God let life form inside me, it had to mean something. The sin was in the sex, never the child. I'd always been heavy-set, so nobody noticed. No cute round bump. Same clothes. Same halls. Same life except my life was changing inside me quietly. I was still going to Largo High, laughing in class, playing it cool, hiding something I hadn't even fully accepted myself. Then the intercom cracked loud like it was calling me out: "Diane White, please report to the office for early dismissal." Early dismissal? For me? My homegirl looked over and whispered, "It's your mother." My mother did not pop up at school. That was unheard of. Instant fear hit my throat like I swallowed a rock. I left class, walked down that hallway, and I swear it felt like the walls were closing in a little. Like every locker was watching me. Like my footsteps were loud. Even the lion statue in the front lobby looked faded, like it had seen this story before.

I walked into the office, and there she was arms crossed, eyes sharp like she could see straight through me. She didn't ask questions. She didn't ask who. She didn't even sit down. She just said, "Come on." We walked outside with cold air, sky gray, and quiet world.

And right there in front of the school doors she stopped, staring at my stomach like it was speaking for me. I was all stomach. And she laughed. That "I knew it" type laugh. Not funny to me. Not even a little. I said exactly how it came out: "This sh*t not funny." Because it wasn't. My childhood was standing on one side of that parking lot and adulthood was calling me to the other.

Our family wasn't traditional. We didn't sit at tables and unpack feelings. We didn't do soft talk. We survived. We adjusted. We kept moving. Love didn't always look gentle. It looked like duty. Presence without conversation. Correction without softness. So, when pregnancy news spread, it wasn't comfortable at first. It was opinions. Judgement. Tongues. My oldest sister, who you'd think would understand as a former teen mom, looked me in my face and told me:

"You fast. You gon' keep having babies. You ain't gon' be nothing but laying on your back. You gon' be on welfare your whole life."

Words cut deeper than labor pains. And they stuck. Haunted me. Followed me. But those same words built something in me too, a fire. Everything she said I silently promised myself I would prove wrong.

Thank God for my middle sister action over emotion, always. No lecture. No panic. No judgement. Just stood with me.

Sometimes presence is louder than advice. And my sister on my father's side? She showed love her own way. She didn't have to care, that baby wasn't hers, but she helped me hustle legally, think smart, learn survival, prepare for the world I was walking into.

Nobody knew how scared I was. Fifteen. Barely understanding myself. Carrying a whole soul with no manual.

But I knew one thing: This baby wasn't a mistake, she was purpose. Due date was March 16. Induced March 15; two months before my sixteenth birthday.

And two weeks before that, I lost my great-grandmother.

I went to her funeral heavy, belly out, sadness sitting in my chest like bricks, people whispering like I couldn't hear judgment through perfume and pews.

But my brother-in-law, God rest his soul took my hand, walked me up to say goodbye to her, walked me back to my seat like security, and sat beside me the whole time. No words just presence.

God spoke through his silence.

At fifteen, I wasn't just pregnant.

I was transforming.

Grieving life lost while carrying life inside me.

Shamed by family but held by God.

Scared but chosen.

I didn't feel ready but purpose don't wait for permission. God already decided I was strong enough.

I remember walking into PG Hospital to be induced. I had heard horror stories about that hospital people talked about it like it was the last place you want to deliver a baby, but I didn't have options. I couldn't pick hospitals, especially when I had hidden my pregnancy almost my entire term, and my doctor delivered there.

All I had was God and the moment.

I settled into the room. The nurse came in and told me I could no longer eat solid food. Just ice chips and water. That's all. Ice. Chips. And water. Kevin, my boyfriend, was there. He said he was going to go talk to his mother. Maybe he did. But when he came back, I swear I smelled Popeyes on his breath, and all I could think was, wow, I'm over here chewing ice while he is out there eating chicken.

Contractions started getting heavy. I never had period cramps, so I didn't know what to compare it to just pain I had never felt before. Deep, pulling, no escape. But the nurse didn't make me feel like a burden. She understood I was young. She could have spoken down to me, judged me, acted like I deserved it, but she didn't. She didn't make me "sit in my consequence." She offered me relief. She asked if I wanted an epidural. Yes. I said yes. They cleared the room. They exposed my back.

I remember sitting still, trying to breathe, trying not to cry, trying to be strong. And the nurse leaned in close, calm, gentle, and whispered: "Deep breath. You're doing fine. You're strong, mama." That moment meant something to me. Not because it was dramatic but because it was real. Because she spoke to me like I mattered.

Like I wasn't just a teen statistic. Like I wasn't a mistake. Like I was a mother. And that was the start of me becoming one. After I had my daughter, life came fast. There was no pause button, no slow introduction into motherhood. One minute I was a 15-year-old girl, and the next I was somebody's mother.

We weren't on our own. We lived with his family. A three-story house with a two-car garage, four bedrooms, three bathrooms and a half bath. Enough room for everybody. Enough space to breathe. Enough walls to hold memories. That house is where my daughter grew up. Her first steps, first words, holidays, birthdays, all of them happened there.

To this day, she calls that place home because it is. It's where she opened her eyes to life. Where she is loved. Where she is covered. I was young, but I was trying.

Going to school, waking up for feedings, juggling homework with bottles and diaper bags. I was learning motherhood at the same time I was still learning myself. But we had help. A family around us, food in the kitchen, people in the house. It wasn't perfect, but it was stable. And stability felt like luxury at that age.

Some mornings I went to school tired trying to stay awake in class while my mind was somewhere between motherhood and math. But I kept going. I didn't drop out. I didn't fold.

I was surviving with a baby on my hip and prayers in my pocket. And somewhere in that routine, God started pulling on me.

We began going to church at Holy House of Praise on Nannie Helen Burroughs in D.C. Sometimes Restoration Kingdom in District Heights. Church wasn't new to me, but the way I needed God now was different. I wasn't just listening to sermons. I was searching. Hungry for peace. Tired from carrying life too young.

Sunday after Sunday I sat in those pews, my daughter in my arms, her father beside me, his family around us. I didn't always shout. I didn't always sing.

Sometimes I just sat there quietly, letting the choir wash over me like water. And then one service shifted everything. No lightning. No preacher calling my name. Just a still moment, like the whole room paused and God leaned close.

Maybe it was a church mother leaning over, maybe it was a whisper in my spirit I can't tell you the exact voice, but I heard it clearly: "Baby, you're safe." Safe.

A word I hadn't felt deeply in a long time. And right there in that sanctuary, tears came. Not because I was weak but because God touched places nobody knew were hurting.

I'd been to church plenty of times growing up, but this time God wasn't a concept He was present. It felt like He wrapped His hand around my heart and said, I see you. I know you. You're still mine. That was the first time I truly felt the blood of the Lord flow through my life for myself not through tradition, not through family expectations, but relationship.

Transition

*And even while God was working on me, life
didn't slow down. I still had a baby girl depending
on me, school to finish, and adulthood knocking
whether I felt ready or not.*

*We were living with his family, and I won't take
that away from them. They stepped in, they made
space for us, they provided what many girls my
age didn't get. There was food in the kitchen, heat
in the winter, laughter in the living room, and a
safety net I needed more than I even understood
back then.*

*But support doesn't mean it was always easy. His
mother loved my daughter fiercely not just as a
grandmother, but as a protector. Overprotective in
a way that came from love, yes but sometimes that
love wrapped tight around postpartum emotions
that I didn't always know how to name or navigate
at fifteen. I was a new mother trying to learn my
baby, while also learning how to share my baby.
She meant well. She still does even now, but some
days it felt like I was proving myself as a mother
in a house where everybody wanted to help raise
what came from my own body.*

*That type of dynamic teaches you early how
motherhood can be lonely even when the room is*

full, that's when I knew the blood of the Lord flowed.

It wasn't anybody else's faith, it was mine. And even with that moment, I still had life happening. Diapers, bottles, school mornings, and a baby depending on me to show up even when I was tired. We were still living with his family. I'll always acknowledge that. They loved us. They fed us. They gave us a place to lay our heads.

But with love comes layers!

His mother was overprotective of her granddaughter still is. And that mixed with my postpartum... whew. Some days I felt supported. Some days I felt watched. Some days I felt like, "I'm her mother too, let me learn." But we were a family.

We were young but we were responsible. No pretending to be grown, we just had to be. He changed pampers. I made bottles. We tag-teamed feedings and late-night cries. We laughed. We made memories. We had good days, real good ones. The kind that makes you believe y'all going to make it.

***But love changes when reality sets in!** At first it was small things such as tone, attitude, little arguments about nothing.*

You ever feel a shift without seeing it? Like, you know, energy is not the same, but you can't prove it.

A woman's intuition is God's private warning system.

I felt unseen sometimes, like I was there physically but low-key invisible emotionally. He would be distant, then close, then distant again. And eventually it wasn't just feelings it was other girls. Texts. Messages. Phone calls that didn't add up. He put his phone face down.

My stomach knew before my eyes. He started checking my phone and I won't act perfect because I started checking his too. Love became a passcode. Trust became something we monitored instead of felt. We both played a part in that downfall. Still, I stayed. Not because I was dumb but because I wanted my family. Because I believed effort could fix what immaturity was breaking. And THIS is where my truth shifts into the part that changed everything...

Chapter 6
The Night, He Woke Me Up

It's crazy how the same hands that once saved you can be the same hands that later hurt you. I'll never forget he was the one who spoke up when that shadow, I mentioned earlier started hovering over me.

But years later, life flipped the story.

That same boy I once felt safe with became the man who broke pieces of me, I didn't even know were still healing. We had been together since middle school. I was around eleven when it started. We grew up together. We laughed, fought, dreamed, and built something that felt like forever. It was the middle of the night. House quiet. Baby finally sleeps and life continues. I was knocked out tired, body heavy, mind finally resting after a long day of bottles, homework, and next thing I know, I feel him shaking me. Not gentle. Not "baby wake up." More like Get up, I got something to show you. Eyes barely open, I'm half confused, half irritated like, "What? What's wrong?"

He is standing over me with my phone in his hand screen lit up bright as day in a dark room. His

*face was already mad and you can see it before he
even speaks. Jaw tight. Breathing heavy. Like he'd
been rehearsing anger while I was sleeping. I
hadn't even checked my phone before bed. Didn't
know what was on it, who texted, nothing. I was
sleeping good too.
You know that deep sleep where your body finally
gets still?
Yeah, that one!
He holds the phone out like evidence, screen right
in my face. "You cheating? You talking to niggas?
What's this?"
My eyes are blurry, trying to adjust, and I saw the
message. It's from my home boy. The gay one,
cool with my cousin playful, silly, harmless as
ever, text saying something like:
"Heyy boo meet me at the lockers." And instantly
my brain like... THIS? This is what you woke me
up out of my sleep for? Meanwhile he been talking
to girls, disappearing, playing hide-and-seek with
loyalty. But I'm the one on trial over a message
from a boy who doesn't even like girls?
I told him "He gay. Chill out." But he heard
nothing. To him, that message meant betrayal. To
him, boo meant I was doing what he had been
doing. It was dumb because I'm me I laughed.*

Sleep still in my eyes, bonnet probably sideways, and I start laughing like: "Boy stop. You really woke me up over THAT?" Real D.C. clowning, not scared, just confused how THIS was the issue. But that laugh? That's what lit the fire.

He told me to, "stop laughing." I didn't. Because the situation was ridiculous. Because I was tired. Because sometimes humor is how we cope with disrespect. He got louder. I sat up. We are face-to-face now. Arguing. Voices bouncing off walls in the dark.

Baby in the other room sleep. Every word felt like scratching an old wound.

And then before I could blink, he swung. Hard. Fast.

Caught me directly in my mouth. Braces cut my gums instantly. Warm blood came quickly. I could taste metal before I could even process pain. My laugh died. Shock hit first. Embarrassment second. Pain third, sharp, burning, pulsing.

The room was still dark, but everything felt loud. Blood on my hand. Tears I didn't want to fall. Everything is blurry; sleep, pain, confusion mixing.

All from a message I didn't even see first. All from a moment I didn't even start. Blood was coming fast, warm, salty, dripping down my lip onto my shirt. My brace wire felt like it was cutting every time I moved my mouth. I put my hand over it, stunned, breath shaky like I was trying to catch up to what just happened.

The room wasn't quiet, it was heavy.

He stood there with that look men get when anger turns into regret mid-action. Like he knew he crossed a line he couldn't uncross. I wasn't screaming. I wasn't even loud.

Sometimes pain makes you silent. It's like the room swallowed sound before it could leave my throat. I think silence is what made everything louder.

Because his mother and stepfather came running, feet on carpet quick, doors swinging open. Lights came on bright, exposing everything, my face, my lip, blood, their son looking like he wished he could rewind time.

His mom's eyes went wide. She grabbed a towel, put it on my mouth, talking fast, panicked, worried you could hear the hurt in her voice. She wasn't choosing sides; she was in shock too.

His stepfather is already grabbing keys, saying, "Come on, we gotta go now." No time to argue. No time to think. Just movement. I remember walking out of that house with blood still dripping,

hands shaking, mouth throbbing, baby still
sleeping in the room down the hall.
That messed with me. Loving somebody and
bleeding in the same night under the same roof,
your child sleeps. The car ride felt long and short
at the same time. I held that towel to my face,
trying not to cry, trying not to swallow blood.
In my head I kept thinking "Over a text? Really?"
Southern Maryland Hospital lights hit me like
reality. They moved me quickly and said I'd need
surgery, root canals, wiring basically
reconstructing my smile.
And all I could think was "Lord, I'm too young for
this." They asked me questions. What happened?
Who hit you? Is he your boyfriend? Do you feel
safe? Do you want to press charges? I'll never
forget what came out my mouth: "Hell nah. I'm
not finna raise this baby by myself." People won't
understand that unless they lived it.
Love. Fear. Survival. Pride. *All mixed up in one*
decision. It wasn't me protecting him. It was me
protecting what I thought was family. What I
hoped could still be fixed.
Then my mama walked in.
Whewwww. Face tight. Eyes fire red. Body was
moving like she was deciding if she was going to
tear the hospital up or drag me home. She looked

*at my mouth, the dried blood, the stitches starting,
and I could see the hurt turn to anger right in her
eyes. She was furious, not just mad, mama furious.
The kind that comes from seeing your baby
harmed. She had every right to be.*

*But in my young mind, things were twisted.
Because I remembered when he protected me from
something she didn't protect me from at first. And
that confusion sat heavily.*

*So, when they asked again about charges. I shook
my head on the stay-away orders. No jail. No
papers. No distance. He wasn't getting off. He was
going to help take care of his daughter.*

*This was a life lesson, not a life sentence. And the
lesson was clear: Keep your damn hands-off
people. Love should never make you bleed.
Arguments shouldn't end in emergency rooms.
And pain doesn't equal passion, it equals
brokenness.*

*What I didn't know then was that this wasn't the
last giant I'd face. It was one battle, but my life
had plenty more lined up. And every time one fell,
another one tried to stand in front of me. Just like
David.*

David & Me
The Giant Slayers

David wasn't the strongest.
He wasn't the biggest.
He wasn't the one people expected to win.
*But he was **the one God chose**.*
While everybody else was trembling in armor,
David stepped forward with nothing but a
slingshot, a stone, and faith that could split
mountains.
Goliath laughed. People doubted. His own
brothers rolled their eyes like, "Who does he think
he is?"
But David knew something they didn't: The battle
was never his; it was God's. And Goliath fell. One
giant. One victory.
One moment that changed everything. But see...
David's story doesn't end at Goliath.
Life kept handing him giant after giant; jealousy,
betrayal, denial, heartbreak, running for his life,
people flipping on him, people lying on him,
battles he never asked for.
Yet every time, God lifted him back up. And
honestly? That's been my life too. I've been
fighting Goliath after Goliath

Family betrayal giants, broken heart giants,
poverty giants, health giants, silent battles nobody
even knew I was carrying.
I didn't have a slingshot, but I had prayer. *I had*
faith.
I had God's hand on my life, even when I felt like I
was drowning.
Like David, I didn't look like the one who would
survive it.
I didn't look like the one who would win in the
end.
But God kept choosing me.
God kept covering me.
God kept strengthening me when I could barely
stand.
People told their side...
People painted their pictures...
People tried to tear me down...
But they forgot something: I sought the heart of
the Lord.
And He's the only one who can save you.
He's the only one who can raise you.
He's the only one who can turn a nobody into His
chosen somebody.
I've fallen.
I've cried.
I've broken. But every single time?

God said, "Get up."
So, I'm telling you the same thing: Get ya ass up.
This giant ain't bigger than your God.
You were built for this battle.
You were chosen for this moment.
And just like David, you're going to look back and say:
"Every giant that came for me fell."

Chapter 7
The Woman Who Raised Me While I Raised Myself

There's a certain silence that comes when you start to tell the truth about your parents. Not the sugar-coated version for Facebook, but the one that still makes your throat tighten a little when you say it out loud.

For a long time, I thought being honest about my childhood meant disrespecting my mother. Now I know it means honoring what we both survived. See, my mother wasn't evil. She was exhausted. She was a woman trying to fill a void while raising children who needed her more than the people she chased. She didn't have a village; she had survival instincts. Sometimes, survival looks selfish when you're the child watching from the corner of the room.

My mama was beautiful and broken at the same time. She was strong enough to hold the house together, but not always strong enough to hold herself. I watched her struggle, not just with bills or heartbreak, but with the weight of choices that

*followed her. The men she loved? Every one of
them fought demons of their own.*

*Addiction had a seat at our table before I ever
knew what the word meant. It showed up in the
way the phone rang late, in the way money
disappeared, in the way her laughter sometimes
carried pain behind it. That's the environment I
came from. It was chaos dressed like normal.
But even though she did her best. She was healing
wounds she never got time to talk about. And
through it all, she still showed up. She still
worked, cooked, laughed, danced, and found ways
to make nothing stretch into something. She
prayed quiet prayers when no one was watching.
Even when she was hurting, she made sure we
were fed, clean, and ready to face the world. My
mama had her battles, but she also had her
brilliance. She had wisdom that came from
surviving.*

*She loved differently because she was loved
differently and yet, that love still found its way to
me. She taught me the kind of strength that doesn't
come from books, the kind of grace that only
comes from walking through fire and choosing not
to let the smoke define you.*

*So yes, I tell the truth, but I tell it with flowers.
Because even through the cracks, she bloomed.*

And she planted that same resilience in me. To this day, we have a great relationship. We laugh, we talk, we heal. I love her deeply, and I cherish every memory we have now, because I've already mourned the version of her, I needed when I was younger. Now I just appreciate the woman she's become.

I had to raise myself emotionally long before I ever became a mother physically and somewhere in the middle of all that growing up too fast, I started noticing pieces of myself that never sat still. The racing thoughts, the half-finished ideas, the days when I could focus for hours and others when my mind felt like static.

Back then, I didn't have a name for it — and even now, I don't know for sure — but I've always wondered if it was a trace of something deeper, something like ADHD showing up before I ever knew what that meant. All I knew was that my brain didn't move in straight lines; it ran like a maze. It's fast, curious, and full of sparks and honestly, I've learned to love that about me. Because maybe God built me that way on purpose to notice what others miss, to juggle ten thoughts at once, and to still find my way back to peace. That's why, when my daughter came, I knew one thing for sure: I was going to protect her the way I wished somebody had protected me.

Looking back now, I see that this was my real test from God. To see if, despite it all, I would still honor my mother and my father. Not because they were perfect, but because they were part of the plan that made me possible. Honoring them doesn't mean pretending the past didn't hurt. It means I can look at it, tell the truth about it, and still choose love when bitterness tries to move in.

*That's **growth.***

*That's **grace.***

That's God.

Chapter 8
Being Everything at Once

Being a mother. Being a student. Being everything at once and still barely knowing who I was outside responsibility. Life was flowing. I was outside of heartbreak, outside of trauma, outside of the version of me that waited to be loved back. And in that healing season life surprised me again.

Before the hotel keys. Before the church leader opened a door. Before God sent strangers to hold me together…let me tell you how I ended up with no address in the first place.

After my brother died, the house wasn't the same. Grief lived there like an unseen roommate. About 6–8 months later, my mom's long-term boyfriend went to jail. Fast-forward to 2017, he comes home. June release. Halfway house. By July he's having visits. Back like he never left. But something was different. Jail had him Bible-thumping and holier-than-thou, but compassion? Grace? Understanding? None. He didn't like the fact I was pregnant. Didn't hide it either. Judged me heavy like I was the only sinner in the room. Like he forgot God saves sinners first, not saints.

Then one day, with a belly full of life inside me, he pretty much said I had to go. Not a suggestion; a decision. And the part that carved something deep in me? My mama stood by him. Didn't stop him. She didn't cover me. Just chose her man over her daughter. That pain? That's the type that sits in your chest years after the moment is gone.

My oldest sister stepped in; not with a room, not with a bed, but with a sentence that changed my future. "Blessed is the child that has they own." At twenty-one years old I finally saw what my sisters lived. The favoritism. The blindness. The way women break their daughters trying to keep men. Her man came home. So, I left.

I am eight months pregnant. Bags in my hand. Pride in my pocket. Peace over chaos. I wasn't staying to argue. I wasn't begging for space in a house where love required permission.

Leaving was painful but staying would've killed parts of me God had plans for. So, I left. And that's how the wilderness started.

I ended up pregnant again. No soft love story. No fairytale. Just real life. Honestly, I got pregnant over the first link. (It be like that sometimes. God's real, hormones realer.)

I won't go deep into baby daddy number two we not giving free chapters where free chapters are not earned. His dad though?

He was a blessing. Even through sickness, he was one of the reasons I kept my baby. A good man at the core. His mother different story. I thought she loved me. Later, I learned she only loved me as long as I was below her. Spoke down on my name like my shine bothered her insecurities. But that's a footnote not a feature. We ain't giving her fame in a book she didn't pour into.

Because the real angels were my daughter's great-grandparents.

Saving grace for real. The support I needed when others failed me.

Wisdom, values, and respect they poured into her what the world couldn't teach. Never charged me daycare, never made me feel like a burden, just loved her, which allowed me work so I could stand on my own feet. They were blessings and blessings don't need paragraphs to prove it. Just recognition. But blessings didn't stop life from life'ing.

Even with love around me, I was still in a season where stability slipped right through my fingers. And although I was growing, healing, hustling that little voice that remembered every insult whispered loud. The "teenage mother who was gonna keep having kids" yeah, that one.

Now here I was pregnant with baby number two at 21, and it was like life was proving them right... or so I thought. But no. I wasn't about to prove them right. I wasn't about to be another story they passed around kitchens and group chats.

I wasn't staying with my second daughter's father, wasn't going back to baby daddy number one, and I was sure as hell wasn't giving my messy family anything else to talk about. Because let's be honest, they already had plenty to say. So no, I wasn't about to prove them right.

I spent a few nights at baby daddy #1's house, a few more sleeping in my car. And those car nights? Whew. When it's just you, your baby, and silence pride hits different.

My pride was huge back then. I couldn't ask for help. I didn't want pity. And deep down, I knew — nobody was coming to save me. It was me. That's it. I had to figure it out. Umm... do I look like a psychic?? ***I didn't have a plan, but I had God.*** *I screamed His name. I mean screamed. I wept. I'm talking tears, snot, the kind of crying where you can't breathe right. I begged Him to show me what to do next. And He did. Not all at once, but piece by piece.*

A church leader stepped in and helped me get a hotel for two months. Two months of a roof over my head. Two months of somewhere safe to lay my baby down. It wasn't fancy, but it was peaceful. It was a door that locked. It was hot water and quiet. It was God saying, I still see you.

Then came this woman from my job. She didn't know me from Adam. Didn't owe me a thing. But she saw my heart. She saw me trying to keep it together when life kept falling apart. She looked at me one day and said, "You and your baby can come stay with me." I ain't gonna lie I was hesitant at first. I wasn't used to kindness that didn't come with strings. But something about her spirit felt safe. So, we went.

She gave us a room. A bed. Hot water. Things people take for granted, but when you've had nothing, they mean everything. That woman didn't know it, but she was the answer to a prayer I cried from the driver's seat of my car at 3 a.m. She gave me hope when I was running on fumes. That moment changed how I saw God.

Because sometimes, the blessing doesn't come from blood. It comes from a stranger with a pure heart. And that's when I learned family ain't always who you're born to. Sometimes it's who God sends when you're too tired to ask for help.

Chapter 9
My First Keys, My First Safe Place

There's nothing like turning a key in a door that got your name on the lease. Not mama's name. Not a boyfriend's name. Not Section 8. Mine. Market rent, $1400 for a one-bedroom. Paraprofessional salary barely touching 40k. Two kids on my hip. School on my back. Covid outside the door like a thief.

But when I walked into that empty apartment, I cried the type of cry that came from your belly. Snot cry. Relief cry. "God, I made it" cry. No couch. No TV. No silverware. Just a key and faith. But I was proud because for the first time in my life, I had a door I could close behind me and call it mine.

And listen, that one-bedroom became a testimony. Not because it was fancy but because I made it stretch like a mother's love. Closet? Room. Living room? Play area and office. Bedroom? Shared until I could figure life out.

I didn't have a nanny it was just me and them babies. Sun up, sundown. Zoom classes in one room, Pampers in the next. Homework on the floor, bottles warming on the stove. Covid had the world shut down but it opened my hustle.

I found a nighttime work-from-home job, clocking in while my kids slept, typing quietly so the keyboard clicks wouldn't wake them. Diapers in the morning. Zoom school, teacher by 8am. Paraprofessional by day. Once they went to sleep, I began my night shift from home. I was mother, teacher, student, worker, cleaner, cook all shifts and no backup.

People think independence is cute until they see the price.

Independence is bills. Independence is tears you wipe alone. Independence is payday hitting Friday and gone Sunday. But I stayed down. And somewhere between Amazon carts and Dollar Tree hacks, I started building. Crafting things. Selling things. Making things stretch. TikTok DIY queen before TikTok was even popular.

Press-ons, décor, hair, anything legal if it brought income, I was on it. Not for luxury but for lights, rent, Wi-Fi so my babies could go to virtual school. That apartment watched me become a woman. It saw me break quietly, pray loudly, and get back up like resurrection was muscle memory.

Growing up wasn't overnight but every bill paid in that apartment was proof that I didn't die in the statistics they wrote for me.

Chapter 10
SMART Goals, Side Hustles & My AA /Era

This is when the level-up got personal. I started writing SMART goals because I was tired of surviving. I wanted to live. Not just dream but plan. Not just talk but execute.

Goal 1: Get my degree.

Goal 2: Build stability.

Goal 3: Heal.

Goal 4: Elevate.

I took pictures every single day to remind myself I was growing, even on days it didn't feel like it. Some days I looked like disappointment. Other days I looked like answered prayers. But I kept going. I got into a new relationship during that time. Two years solid.

Thought it was love until it wasn't. He had potential just not discipline. He wanted to be better, but he wanted it handed to him. Forgot to mention the part where grown men can still wet beds and since we are telling stories, tell it all. I won't give him too many pages no free meals here. Just know when it ended, I didn't collapse I already knew how to stand. I learned to maintain what was mine without a man holding the other end. I budgeted. I stretched paychecks. I fed kids before I fed my emotions.

And in the midst of broken hearts, bills, and blessings I earned my AA in Teacher Education. The same girl they said would drop out. The same teen mom they whispered about. The fast one. The one "who gon' keep having babies." Degree in hand. Kids in the crowd. God clapping the loudest. That one-bedroom turned into a launchpad.

Where I healed.

Where I prayed.

Where I hustled.

Where I mothered.

Where I passed classes at 2am, sleepy but determined. That apartment was the womb of my becoming. Because nobody saved me. I saved myself. Baby, once you learn how to do that? You become unstoppable. When I was baptized, I was born again. Now everybody left the chat. Let's clear the air this book is a rollercoaster because life is. God uses His strongest soldiers for a reason.

Chapter 11
The Water Knew My Name

I didn't walk into that baptism wearing white like tradition expects I wore black. Some would've called it untraditional, but honestly, it fit. Black like the chapters I survived, black like the weight I carried silently, black like the battles only God and I knew about.

I wasn't there to appear holy. I was there to be healed. There was something symbolic about it, even if I didn't understand it fully then. Black felt like the closing of a chapter, like everything heavy was walking into that water with me.

*I remember stepping in my heart racing, hands cold, spirit wide open. The pastor spoke, but my soul was louder. It was like God whispered, **"This is not performance, this is redemption."** When they lowered me under, the world muffled like sound disappeared and only spirit spoke. It felt like God held me there a second longer, long enough for every silent scream I never released to finally loosen its grip.*

When I came up, the air hit differently. Sharp like clarity, warm like grace, new like fresh breath I didn't know I was missing. People clapped. Some smiled. Pictures were taken. It looked like a moment, but it was a rebirth.

I was strong in public, calm even. But when the night came, when the room got quiet and it was just God and me, I cried. Not for minutes. All night. Tears fell like a flood I had been holding back for years. Pain released, relief, unanswered questions, all pouring out through swollen eyes and shaking breath.

It wasn't sadness, it was soul-laundering. It felt like God was sitting with me on that bed, not condemning me, not reminding me of failures just holding me. No pastor. No choir. No altar call. Just me, my pillow soaked, and Heaven in the room.

That's when I knew: the water touched more than my skin; it touched my destiny.

I didn't just come up wet; I came up claimed.
Chosen, Covered, Called. *I realized God never took His hand off me. Even when I drifted. Even when I ran. Even when life bruised me purple His grip never loosened.*

The baptism was not the start of my gift it was the moment I recognized it. ***I Didn't Choose the Gift It Chose Me.*** *How God marked me quietly long before I understood the calling. I don't need a* *robe, a mic, or a title for God to speak through me. My anointing wasn't handed to me by people it was breathed into me by God.*

I may not carry the title "Prophet" officially, but I move prophetically with vision, discernment, and divine knowing. I am evidence that God does not wait for ordination to choose someone.

I didn't wake up one day calling myself prophetic life revealed it to me before I ever had the language. It was the way my spirit spoke before my mouth ever did.

The way I could walk into a room and feel what wasn't being said. The way God would tug on my chest about people, places, and choices and later it would unfold exactly how He whispered it to me. Not in a spooky way. Not in a "I see angels in the kitchen" way. But in a knowing.

A knowing that didn't come from experience, books, or advice but from something higher, something holy, something woven in me long before I learned how to pray with grown-woman faith.

I have always seen things before they happened. When spirits shift, I feel it. When people's hearts change, mine aches. When something isn't right, my body reacts, my peace leaves, my sleep gets loud.

Discernment for me isn't a Bible verse it's oxygen. Some people talk to hear themselves. I speak when God nudges. Sometimes through warning. Sometimes through humor. Sometimes through a single sentence that stops a soul in its tracks. I don't just read people. I read their wounds, even when they hide them well. I read their silence, their eyes, their energy, their heaviness. And instead of judging it, I sit with it. Hold it. Mirror it back with love. That's prophetic. Prophetic isn't always preaching. Sometimes it's presence. Sometimes it's the ability to pull the real out of somebody.

To make people uncomfortable enough to grow and safe enough to heal at the same time. It's the way strangers tell me their life story in line at the grocery store. The way God gives me words for others that I didn't rehearse. The way my pain became ministry not by choice, but by assignment. I don't call myself a prophet. Titles don't make me. What makes me is the evidence:

• The dreams that warned me before storms hit.
• The intuition that saved me from rooms I didn't belong in.
• The burden I feel before God shifts me to intercession.
• The way peace confirms and chaos convicts.

• The way God uses my life as a testimony in real time.
I'm not perfect but I'm chosen.
Not polished but purpose picked.
Not holy because I pretend, but holy because God kept His hands on me even when I fell. If prophetic means hearing God in whispers, feeling people's pain in my bones, seeing beyond faces into souls, being the mirror nobody asked for but everybody needed. Then yes...There's a prophetic call stitched into my destiny. Not loud, not flashy but real.
I am evidence that God speaks through the overlooked. I am proof that sensitivity is a calling, not a curse. I am what happens when a woman survives her own storms and still stands as light. When the Writing Was Done, I Was Not the Same. Finishing this book didn't feel like typing the last sentence it felt like closing a door gently, turning around, and meeting myself on the other side. By the time I reached these pages, I had cried a little, grown a lot, and let memories rise from places I buried them like old bones.
I wrote through shaking hands some days, through holy fire on others. Some chapters healed me. Some hurt me. Some reminded me that I am still a work in progress and still a masterpiece at the

same time. I didn't just write a story. I gained self-awareness and recognized that my younger self was entitled to compassion.

The woman I am now deserved celebration. And the woman I'm becoming? She deserves room. This book forced me to sit with versions of myself I outgrew, the ones I abandoned, ignored, or powered through because survival didn't leave time for softness.

But here in these closing pages I finally breathe. Not the short breaths I took when life was loud, but a full inhale of understanding. A slow exhale of release. I survived what tried to silence me. I wrote what I used to only think. I faced what I used to avoid. I named what I used to numb. I stood tall in places where I once shrunk. And through every sentence, **God reminded me. You are becoming. You are unfolding.** *You are shedding old skins without apology. You are stepping into purpose with clarity.*

This book caused tension internally, spiritually, and relationally. It stirred things. Exposed things. Pulled truth out of me like splinters. But I'm glad it did. Because peace built on lies isn't peace, it's prison. I refuse to live in chains disguised as silence.

So yes, some pages were heavy. Some confessions were uncomfortable. Some truths shook rooms. But, healing rarely whispers, sometimes it roars. To write this, I had to break open. To finish it, I had to heal. And now, at the end, I feel lighter not because everything is perfect, but because nothing is hidden.

This book didn't just tell my story, it freed it. Now, as I stand at the end of these pages, I realize something beautiful:

I didn't just write a book. I wrote my way back to myself.

If you've read this far, thank you for holding space for my becoming. For witnessing me. For seeing me. For listening to what my soul whispered when my mouth was finally ready to speak. This isn't the end, just the completion of one chapter of me. And I'm proud of her every version. Every scar. Every lesson. Every rise.

The words are finished, but the woman is still unfolding. I used to think all this pain was random.

A daddy who chose addiction over presence. A family that made me pay for sins I didn't commit.

A brother whose life ended in a headline instead of a wedding speech.

A cousin who turned a safe house into a haunted one.
A baby belly showing before my sixteenth birthday.
Eight months pregnant with nowhere to go.
Hotels, cars, couches, and prayers that sounded more like, "Lord, please don't forget me."
A sister gone too soon.
A mama grieving in slow motion.
Heartbreak after heartbreak.
Restart after restart.
I thought it was chaos.
But standing here now as an educator, mother, believer, author, concrete and all, I know better.
It was construction.
I look back at that little girl with the marble notebooks and the fat cheeks, trying to make everybody laugh so nobody saw she was hurting... and I want to hug her.
She thought she was dirt something people walked on, molded, stepped in, tracked through the house and washed off when they were done. She thought being overlooked meant she wasn't enough. She didn't know yet that God was already pouring concrete. She didn't know that every crisis had a purpose attached.

"In this world you will have tribulations. But take heart; I have overcome the world." That's not just a cute scripture to me. That's my life in one sentence. God never told me I wouldn't go through it. He told me I'd never go through it alone.

From the Section 8 apartment to the cul-de-sac house. From the fifth-grade phone pictures of my brother to the call that he got shot. From my mama laid out in depression to me at ten yelling, "I'm still here!"

From being touched when I should've been protected to having a boyfriend and his mama believe me when others remained silent.

From walking through the halls of Largo High with secrets on my shoulders to walking into PG Hospital at fifteen, belly full of baby and fear.

From "no address" to "just faith" and God sending church folk and coworkers to open doors my last name couldn't.

I see it now: every crisis looked like a breaking, but it was really a building.

The Bible doesn't lie about storms. It doesn't sugarcoat the valley. It literally says, "When you pass through the waters, I will be with you... when you walk through the fire, you will not be burned." (Isaiah 43:2)

Not if. When. He knew the flood was coming. He also knew I would survive it.

I passed through waters of grief when they lowered my brother into the ground.

I passed through waters of shame when family judged my belly before they ever prayed for my baby.

I passed through waters of rejection from the whole side of family that chose pride over relationship.

I passed through waters of heartbreak when love was both my comfort and my wound.

I passed through waters of homelessness when my body was a home for life, but I didn't have a home to lay it down in.

And every single time, when I thought I would drown, something, someone showed up.

A nurse whispering, "You're strong, mama," in a cold hospital room. A brother-in-law taking my hand at my great-grandmother's funeral.

A coworker offering help when they didn't have to. A church mother pressing a little money in my hand and saying, "God sees you, baby."

A principal, a professor, a mentor speaking life into my calling when I was ready to shrink.

People will call it coincidence.

*I call it **God in the details.***

Crisis taught me to pray for real. Not the cute prayers. Not the "God is great, God is good" church prayers. I'm talking the ugly cry, "Lord, if you don't do it, it won't get done" kind of prayers. Crisis taught me faith is not denial, it's decision. Decision to believe when nothing looks like the promise. Decision to keep going when your body says quit. Decision to trust God with the parts of the story that still don't make sense.

Crisis taught me endurance. It taught me how to show up for my students when my heart was breaking at home. It taught me how to parent my girls with intention, so they never have to wonder if they are wanted. It taught me how to say "no" without explaining, how to guard my peace like it's sacred which it is. It taught me how to let go of tables that were never built for me and build my own instead.

Crisis taught me I am not dirt anymore. I am concrete. Concrete doesn't mean hard-hearted. It means set. Set in who I am. Set in Whose I am. Set in my assignment. I used to be the girl who stayed in rooms God told me to leave.

The girl who let people plant themselves in my life and treat my heart like soil digging, taking, reshaping, leaving holes. The girl who carried everybody's secret, everybody's crisis, everybody's emotions, while her own soul begged for rest.

Now? I know my boundaries are holy. I know my peace is not a group project. I know I don't have to shrink so others feel tall. I know I am **Overlooked but Chosen**. *You thought you ignored me. God was hiding me. You thought you were hurting me. God was hardening the foundation. When I finally sat with no noise, no audience, no armor and said, "God, I am tired. I have tried it my way. Here I am." He didn't shame me. He didn't say, "I told you so." He leaned in. Sometimes your surrender is the deliverance. Sometimes your "Yes, Lord" is the key that unlocks the life you were always supposed to live. So, what does Built from the Concrete really mean? It means I am the product of every storm I have survived. It means I am the woman that grew out of the dirt they threw on me. It means I am proof that crisis doesn't cancel calling. I am a mother who loves her daughters the way she deserved to be loved. I am an educator who sees the overlooked child in the back of the class because I was her. I am a believer who has receipts with God, not just religion.* **I am** *a writer telling the truth they tried to bury. I am a woman who has cried in showers, car rides,* *and parking lots and still shows up with a smile and a sharp tongue and a soft heart. I am the baby they didn't plan. The teen mom they counted out. The Black sheep they whispered about. The church girl who saw too much. The woman who kept going anyway.*

And through every single crisis, God was there:
* *When my father chose the drug over the daughter.*
* *When my brother's blood hit D.C. concrete.*
* *When hands touched me that shouldn't have.*
* *When I walked school halls pregnant with shame.*
* *When the hotel room became home.*
* *When grief sat on my chest at funerals I didn't want to attend.*
* *When my own body felt like my enemy.*
* *When I thought, "Lord, why me?" and heaven whispered back, "Because you're strong enough to carry it and soft enough to use it."*

So, this is me giving God His flowers while I can still smell mine. He took a chubby girl from around the way, with a last name nobody wanted to claim, and turned her into a woman with a story that breaks chains.

Chapter 12
When Breath is Borrowed

There are moments in life you never rehearse for. Moments that tear the air from your chest and make time feel like it's standing on your shoulders.

I thought I was ready to release my book ready to talk about childhood, trauma, survival, womanhood, and every brick I had to climb over just to breathe. I had my chapters outlined, my title dancing in my notes like it was waiting on me. I was ready to speak on the overlooked child, the unseen daughter, the Black sheep that learned how to love herself in the dark.

Then November 20th, 2025, came and sat in my lap like a scream I couldn't swallow.

My sister collapsed.

Cardiac arrest. Seizure.

Eight minutes without oxygen.

Hospital.

Machines.

The constant chorus of beeping machines filled the room and smelled like bleach and prayers.

Doctors talking in circles that don't feel like English.

And there she was, my sister, breathing but gone. It felt like God pressed pause on my release date and said, "Write this chapter too. Finish what life is still teaching you."

Movement without mind. Life without living. They removed the ventilator Saturday at noon. She kept breathing. Not because she was fighting but because the brainstem knows routine even when the soul has already packed its bags. Breathing became a beat. Steady. Silent. Stealing time. Hospice. Comfort care. Words I never wanted to learn how to pronounce without choking. People think breathing means hope. I learned breathing also means borrowed time. That the body can live after the mind is gone. That the heart can pump after farewell. That the lungs will rise even when the soul is resting. That broke me open. This chapter wasn't planned but it's necessary.

I learned something while writing this book. Some chapters we choose. Some chapters choose us. This one walked in uninvited. Sat on the front row and grabbed my pen with hands I couldn't stop shaking. I had to learn that family stories don't always end how we want. We don't get to rewrite real life only document the truth of it.

The truth is: Sometimes we love people who are already gone emotionally or spiritually long before their body lets go. Sometimes we hold on to relationships that expired years ago out of guilt, habit, or history. Sometimes God makes you finish a chapter even while you're crying through it. And sometimes, no matter how much it hurts you must let the page turn.

Closure isn't betrayal, it's survival. I wanted happy endings with every family member. I wanted forgiveness to be ribboned in gold. I wanted "we made it" stories. I wanted us whole. But life made me understand. Some chapters aren't meant to be stretched into sequels. Some bonds teach you strength, not longevity. Some love stories end quietly not with fireworks, but with a deep exhale. Closure sometimes looks like a hospital room where breath is present, but the person isn't. It took losing my sister in real time breathing yet unreachable for me to understand that letting go is still love. Not the kind where you walk away angry.

But the kind where you place a blanket over someone's story and whisper, "You can rest now. I'll carry the memory." I thought my book was finished.

But grief edits in ink. Maybe this chapter isn't just hers. Maybe it's mine. Maybe it's every person I've ever had to love and release. Every piece of family I had to accept as they were, not as I dreamed them to be. Every goodbye that didn't ask for permission. Death physical or emotional teaches the same lesson: You can't hold what God is asking you to let go of.

Sometimes closure means writing it down, so it doesn't haunt you anymore.

To my sister and every broken tie, I've had to heal from:

*Your breath may fade from earth, but your chapter will live here between my pages, between my ribs, between lessons I earned with tears. You taught me that life is fragile. That love is not always enough to save a body. That **presence is temporary, but impact is permanent.** And though my heart is heavy, I honor this chapter painful, unfinished, and unforgettable.*

Because even in loss, there is growth. Even in grief, there is clarity. Even in silence, love speaks loudly. I release you. I thank you. I carry you. And I turn the page.

Before I could bloom, I had to learn how to stand tall even when life tried to bury me. The confidence I wear now came from surviving storms I never thought I'd make it through. Every smile you've seen wasn't always joy; sometimes it was armor. I took pictures every day, not for attention, but for accountability proof that I was still showing up. Every snapshot became therapy, a way to breathe through what couldn't be explained. What looked like posing was really healing in progress. Each click of that camera caught a moment I refused to hide anymore. For years they overlooked the woman behind the smile, the one who carried the weight, stayed quiet, and still showed up. But now? Now they must watch. Every post, every frame, every angle is not for validation, it's proof. Proof that faith works. Proof that God restores. Proof that confidence can be rebuilt from the concrete. This isn't about being seen, it's about being remembered. About turning pain into presence, and silence into a statement. At the end of each year, I look back and realize how much I've poured into others while barely counting a handful who truly showed up for me. Back then, I didn't understand the process, but now I see it was preparation. Because when they overlooked the story, God made sure they couldn't overlook the glow.

Epilogue
Built from the Concrete

If you had met me when I was quiet, overlooked, and surviving, you might've mistaken me for small. You might've thought I was the statistics they whispered about. Teen mother. Too loud. Too emotional. Too much. Not enough. But you would've been wrong.

*Because I am not what people projected onto me in their discomfort. I am not what trauma tried to reduce me too. I am not the rumors, the labels, the side-eye, or the versions of me people created to make sense of my resilience. I am what God chose. I am a **Black woman** who survived things meant to silence her and still learned how to speak with authority. I am a **HBCU graduate**, built in rooms that taught me pride, discipline, and how to walk in spaces like I belong because I do. I am **an educator**, standing in front of children who look like me, who come from concrete just like I did, reminding them daily that where you start does not get the final say.*

*I am a **motivational speaker**, not because I chased a stage, but because life forced me to find* *my voice and once, I did, I refused to mute it again. Most importantly, **I am a mother.** A girl mom. Two daughters who are watching me more closely than they will ever admit. Watching how I heal. Watching how I love. Watching how I recover. Watching how I refuse to shrink. Watching how I choose myself and still choose them. Everything I've survived, I survived with them in mind even before I knew their names. There were seasons when I felt invisible. Times when being overlooked felt like rejection instead of protection. But now I understand something I couldn't see back then: God hides His chosen ones while He's building them.*

Nobody saw the late nights. Nobody saw the tears in the car. Nobody saw the prayers whispered through clenched teeth. Nobody saw the moments I wanted to quit but didn't. They only saw the outcome and tried to rewrite the process. But I know the truth. I know what it took to get here. Being overlooked didn't break me, it prepared me. It taught me discernment. It taught me boundaries. It taught me how to sit alone without feeling lonely. It taught me how to build when nobody was clapping. When God finally lifted me, the same concrete that tried to bury me became the foundation I stood on.

So, if you're reading this and you've ever felt unseen, unheard, or misunderstood let me tell you what I had to learn the hard way: God does not overlook you. He prepares you. You don't need their approval. You don't need their apology. You don't need their permission. You just need to keep going.

I am no longer trying to prove anything. I don't argue with opinions that don't feed me. I don't audition for rooms that can't hold my presence. I stand in who I am fully, honestly, and without apology.

From overlooked to chosen.

From surviving to standing.

From concrete to calling.

And this?

This is only the beginning.

Acknowledgment
The Hands That Held Me

*"Whom God calls; He also predestines." This
journey would be incomplete without
acknowledging the people who held me up when I
was learning how to stand. I'm careful with my
words, but I believe in giving flowers while people
can still smell them.*

*To the infamous music teacher your kindness was
God's reminder that favor can wear a smile.
Every encouraging word, every laugh, every hug
carried me through more than you knew. You were
light on days that felt heavy, a steady rhythm when
my life felt offbeat. You were grace in human
form, and I will always thank you for that.*

*To my favorite math teacher, C.C., my "mama."
You met me as a young lady and helped me grow
into a grown woman. You taught me how a woman
should think of herself, love herself, and walk
confidently in who she is—without apology. You
didn't just teach math; you taught history, self-
worth, discipline, and life, all in one breath.
You showed me that intelligence is power, that
knowledge is freedom, and that a woman can be*

brilliant, grounded, and yes, sexy all at the same time. You modeled that with ease.

When I got my first apartment, you and your mother showed up with everything I needed, making sure I wasn't just surviving but settling into stability. You fed me, clothed my baby, corrected me when I needed it, challenged me when I tried to shrink, and loved me without conditions. Thank you for being the woman who never needed applause to make an impact yet changed my life simply by being present.

To my Coppin sister, A.B. *- You came into my life real and raw, with no judgment attached. No filters. No expectations. Just truth. You didn't flinch at my story; you sat in it with me. You prayed with me sometimes quietly, sometimes out loud, sometimes in the middle of the storm. You pulled up when things were heavy, stayed when it got uncomfortable, and never asked me to explain myself.*

You didn't try to fix me. You stood with me. You reminded me who I was when I forgot. Somewhere between the prayers, the check-ins, and the moments where life felt like too much, you stopped being a friend and became my sister. Blood couldn't have made us closer. You are genuine, solid, and God-sent and I will always honor you for that.

To my Towson/football sister, M.S. - Thank you for never passing judgment and for always being a voice of reason when emotions tried to take control. You listened without interrupting, spoke truth without tearing me down, and grounded me when life felt chaotic. You reminded me to think clearly, move wisely, and stay rooted in who I am. Your calm, consistency, and honesty meant more than you probably know. Thank you for being steady when I needed balance.

To my twin, A.Y - You prayed for me, covered me, and corrected me with love. Our kids became best friends, and your family embraced mine like their own. From late-night braids to homework help, your presence showed me how intentional God truly is. This one's for you, twin always.

To my best friend, D.W. - Thank you for choosing me every single day, even when life was life-ing. Thank you for your gentleness, your softness with me, and your ability to love without judgment. You never clipped my wings. You encouraged me to fly. You allowed me to chase my dreams without regret, and you helped me build a legacy worth sharing. I don't take that lightly.

To my best friend, D.S. - *The one and only. Life pulled us in different directions for a while, but we never missed a beat maybe skipped one but never lost the rhythm. If anyone can validate this book and the real-life experiences inside these pages, it's you. We were teen moms, trying to survive and make sense of adulthood in real time. You were a sound voice then, and you're still a sound voice now. You know my heart. Here's to beating the odds together.*

And finally, to every colleague and staff member I've worked alongside in Prince George's County Public Schools, thank you. Thank you for showing me exactly who you are, both genuine and the disingenuous. Every encounter taught me something—about people, purpose, boundaries, and protection. You gave me material, and in return, I told my story.

Made in the USA
Middletown, DE
17 January 2026

27238298R00061